GANGS, DRUGS AND VIOLENCE: CHICAGO STYLE

Fourth Edition

JESSE BECKOM JR.

Gangs, Drugs and Violence Prevention Consultants, Inc. Chicago, Illinois

Published by Gangs, Drugs and Violence Prevention Consultants, Inc., P.O.Box 288833, Chicago, IL 60628-8833

Internet address: gdvpc@moon.igcom.net

Visit the Gangs, Drugs and Violence Prevention Consultants Web Page at http://www.ujamma.com/

International Standard Book Number: 0-9645051-0-X
Library of Congress Catalog No.: 95-094135

Printed in the United States of America
Fourth Printing September 1996

Cover illustration by Jesse Beckom III
Photography by Ken Booker
Edited by Kimberly Vann
Designed and printed by If It's Printable...
Chicago, Illinois

DEDICATION

I dedicate this book/manual to my wife, Addie, who has always been there at my side going through the hard times and the good times. She always gave me that extra bit of assistance whenever I needed it, especially during all of the long nights when we stayed up discussing what and how the information should go into the book. And, above all, I thank her for giving me the idea of writing the book so that people could be more informed about gangs. Thanks, baby.

Table of Contents

A candid discussion about how gangs operate, their word usage, signs, codes and the disruption they cause in Chicago and surrounding communities. Includes a graphic pictorial presentation about gang signs and graffiti.

Includes descriptions of various drugs sold by gangs and a look at how certain drugs are used and how to tell if someone is using them.

Examines how gang violence impacts victims and their families. Also provides common-sense safety tips.

Table of Contents cont.

FOREWORD

Any effort to confront and impact a problem must begin with a diagnosis...so must efforts to solve or, at least, influence a social problem begin with an understanding of that problem. With that in mind, over the years Americans have unconsciously conducted a war on problem solving. They have listened and followed the dictates of the erudite academician and the theorist...but over the years, these problems have escalated. They have listened and followed the proposed directions of men of good will, but men who have seldom walked in the moccasins of those they attempt to change.

Now we have a chance to stimulate our problem solving machinery by studying the malady from within...from a man who cries on the inside when he sees what is happening to the youth of America. Jesse Beckom has been there. He is on a mission which began in the bowels of the cancer which has spread across much of our country. He is a veteran Chicago Policeman and he has influenced the lives of more teenagers with firm kindness and understanding than any lawman has done with a gun and club. Jesse Beckom's text on GANGS, DRUGS AND VIOLENCE is a must for anyone who is concerned about the health and safety of everyone who walks the streets of AMERICA.

Russ Ewing

II

ACKNOWLEDGMENTS

I would like to acknowledge the following people and organizations whose unconditional support and encouragement were instrumental in making my dream of writing this manual become a reality:

My wife, Addie, and my children, Venus, Jesse III and Ulanka; my mother, Catherine; my former partners, Darnell Ross and John Blackman; my favorite elementary school teacher, Nathaniel Blackman; Mrs. Austin and Mrs. Kyles, Nansen Elementary School and Coach Loftus, Corliss High School.

I also want to give thanks to a person who is no longer with us: Mayor Harold Washington. I had the pleasure of serving as a member of his executive security team. From him, I learned patience and understanding. Through him, I became a better person, watching how he gave of himself limitlessly.

INTRODUCTION

I have been a Chicago police officer for 25 years, during which time I received 56 honorable mentions from the Chicago Police Department and 10 letters of recommendation from private citizens. During the early part of my career I worked in the Fillmore neighborhood in the 11th District. I handled liquor law violations, narcotics, prostitution and gambling cases. As my career progressed, I gained firsthand information and experience with gang activities, after which I became a part of the tactical unit in the 3rd District. There I handled in-progress calls such as burglary, robbery, homicide and sex crimes.

I was then assigned to the Special Operations Group (S.O.G.) South, which is now known as the Gang Crimes - South Unit. The unit consisted of a team of 14 - 15 officers, a sergeant and lieutenant. Our mission was to saturate and patrol high-crime areas in certain districts, sometimes in civilian dress and unmarked vehicles.

After leaving that unit, I was assigned to the Museum of Science and Industry, Beat 331-a. I served and met at least 15,000 - 20,000 people a day in Jackson Park, the inner and outer harbors, La Rabida Medical Center, Jackson Park golf course, driving range, soccer fields, Jackson Park beach, Omnimax Theater and the South Shore Country Club. These areas were home to a high level of gang activity.

In my next assignment, I served as a bodyguard for former Mayor Harold Washington. After his death, I became a bodyguard for former Mayor Eugene Sawyer. In 1990 I was assigned to the Public Transportation detail at 95th and the Dan Ryan "El", one of the busiest locations in Chicago, where I had weekly contact with up to 1.5 million people. The station is the end of the "El" and bus lines on the city's south limits. Students from various elementary and high schools, including Phillips, Dunbar, DuSable, Tilden, Hyde Park, Englewood, Kenwood, Mother McCauley, Brother Rice, Corliss, Fenger, Julian, Harlan, De La Salle and St. Martin

DePorres used the CTA's south rapid transit system. I worked at the 95th Street terminal between 1990 and 1992, and I could not help but become very conscious of gang activities, considering someone had to talk to the young people to make them understand that the police were on their side. Unfortunately, approximately 15 - 20 arrests per month had to be made for drugs and for weapons ranging from 22 automatics to 9 mm guns.

I, along with my partner, received an award from our unit for having the highest arrest activity record. After arresting so many people in a year's time, I found that most of the young people were not gang members but, in fact, were carrying weapons for their own protection. This was later substantiated by court records that stated 70 percent of these young people had no prior arrest records. Realizing that the gang situation was coming to a head made me see that I was correct in my reason for becoming a police officer.

Police officers are the first line of protection for a young person between life in the criminal justice system or life as a constructive, productive citizen. One should use this highly visible position to serve as a role model, because without guidance and direction, most young people become susceptible to peer pressure. As a police officer, you can give them leadership and serve as a positive image. I felt it would be best to try to redirect some of the young people. I came out of the Ida B. Wells projects, on Chicago's South Side, and understood the benefits of staying out of a gang. I felt that by being a police officer, I could try to reach out and help someone who was in a situation or being forced into a situation they could no longer control or were afraid to do anything about. It was for this reason, and this reason alone, that I became a police officer. In this position, you must try and change a person's attitude, even if they don't think it is part of your job to do so.

One day while working at 95th and the Ryan, this young man came through the terminal. He was about 16 and was using profanity, loudly and descriptively telling his friend how he had sex with a female. I stopped him and stated that he could not use that type of profane language in public and that he was disrespecting the females, an offense for which he could be arrested for disorderly conduct and putting the citizenry in fear for their safety. After my remarks, the teenager became even louder and started attracting a crowd of people. He went on to say that this was his mouth and he could say what the f— he wanted.

I then asked him his age and what school he attended. He said he was a junior at Paul Robeson and was 16 years old. I asked if he knew who Paul Robeson was. He answered by saying "Yes, Paul Robeson was a basketball player for the Knicks." While all the questioning was going on, a lady was standing next to us, looking at me with a big smile on her face. I proceeded to tell the young man that Robeson was the best African-American opera singer that the United States has ever produced, that he graduated from college summa cum laude and that he excelled as an athlete in basketball, baseball and track. But he did not play basketball for the Knicks. I looked at the lady standing nearby, and the smile on her face grew larger by the moment.

At this point, I asked the young man what were they teaching him at Robeson and if he knew anything about fractions? He quickly replied, "I don't break any legs." The lady started laughing loudly and said the teenager and I would make a great comedy team. I then asked him which denomination he was. This time, he answered quicker than ever and said he was broke. The lady started laughing hysterically and walked away, slightly bent over from the laughter.

After this outburst, I took the teenager into the back room where we had a long and interesting conversation about his use of language in public. I then returned him to the terminal area and sent him on his way with a different attitude about how he should conduct himself.

Several years later, I met that same young man at a gas station. He remembered me and told me I had scared the hell out of him and from then on, his life had gone in a different direction. He told me he was graduating from Alabama State College and that he owed it all to the conversation that we had years earlier at the terminal. Then he thanked me for my help. This story shows you that most young adults are just looking for a little help and understanding and someone to talk to them with respect. I know for a fact that the young adults are fed up with the gang activity. They can't go to the parks, beach, playgrounds or just hang out playing basketball without somebody coming around with a 40-ounce and trying to start a fight over nothing.

During the writing of this book--a 26-year effort--I established the purpose and ideals that I am trying to impart to teachers, young people and parents who understand the seriousness of gangs, drugs and violence. In doing so, for the past six years I have delivered informative presentations on gangs, drugs and violence prevention to a wide range of audiences. These include various churches, organizations, elementary and high schools, teachers at in-service workshops and some 20,000 students. In 1992, my wife and I started Gangs, Drugs and Violence Prevention Consultants to impart much-needed knowledge and insight to people in both beleaguered and relatively violence-free communities.

Together we can--and will--make a difference.

GANGS, DRUGS AND VIOLENCE:
CHICAGO STYLE

Chapter 1
GANGS

There is a war going on in this modern, technology-oriented society called the United States of America. You don't have to go to Ireland and deal with the Protestants and the Catholics. You don't have to go to Beirut and deal with the Palestinians or the Israelites. Nor do you have to go to Bosnia and face the Muslims or the Croatians. The only difference in the wars going on in those countries and the war in the United States is that the young gang members are waging war in varying locations.

You can step outside of any door anywhere and become a statistic of gang violence. At least in other countries you know in what areas the wars are taking place. In America's wars, you must be well informed about what to look out for in order not to become a statistic of gang violence. These days, you can walk or drive your car in the wrong area and be mistaken for a gang member. The only way to survive in the streets is for everyone to become more informed about gangs and their activities. That means knowing about gang colors, gang signs, gang actions and gang boundaries.

Presently there is a change taking place in the gangs and that change is for the better. Young people between the ages of 15 and 20 are raising their younger sisters and brothers, telling them to stay out of gangs, stay away from drugs and stay in school. This group is doing so because they have seen how quickly street life destroys. Sadly enough, their parents are too busy trying to get material things like cars, homes, clothes, jewelry, etc. But parents, for the most part, do not know what to look for regarding gangs and they don't take time to find out basic gang information.

Teachers are on the frontlines of the wars with gangs because they are being forced to become mothers and fathers to our youth. The teachers spend more time with young people during six and a half hours of school than the parents. The only other person that may spend more time with young people is another young person, usually someone in their peer group.

Within the next two years there will be a drop in gang activity because of young people changing their younger sisters' and brothers' attitude toward gangs. So the logical answer to the problem of gangs is to encourage young people to lead young people as the schools are trying to do. With the help of the adult population, this change could be realized more quickly.

There is a white gang known as the Skinheads (SH) who have a nationwide following with local members located in the far southwest and northwest suburbs of Chicago. This gang advocates white power and has been known to start fights with anyone of color. Male members sometimes shave their heads bald and the females have been known to cut the hair around the sides of their head and letting the hair hang long, camouflaging the area cut. Skinheads recruit by instilling fear in other Caucasians and forcing them to join for their safety. There also is a group of African Americans, Caucasians, Hispanics and other people of color who call themselves the "Antis" and who are against the Skinheads. Thus far, there have been few problems between the Skinheads and the Antis.

The weapons that most gangs have are being sold to them after being taken in a burglary from an apartment or home in the city or outlying areas. Therefore, the citizenry is unknowingly providing the gangs with the weapons. Almost 80 percent of all the weapons that I have recovered from criminals were found to have been taken in burglaries. If you want to know how many weapons are in the city and other areas, just listen to the shots being fired on New Year's Eve and the Fourth of July. Gangs in Chicago have always been well-rooted in society, even more so than Al Capone and other ruthless people.

Youth today are drawn to gangs because of three new factors: drugs, money and rapid-fire weapons. The first thing that must be understood is that the gangs and young people we are dealing with today are highly intelligent. They are not stupid; they do stupid things. A dumb person does dumb things: a smart person does stupid things. It must also be noted that most young people do not belong to gangs. I would say 85 percent of the young people out there do not belong to gangs in Chicago. Of the 15 percent who do, approximately 5 percent are hardcore young people who have dropped out of school but will hang around a school.

There is another 10 percent who will follow along behind that 5 percent of so-called gang members and who might be in school but, upon exiting school, try to hang with the gang members. It is unfortunate that in our society those gang members who participate in criminal activity are highly visible and get all of the attention. In trying to illustrate some of the activities, codes, understanding and knowledge I have obtained about gangs, let me first say to the parents and teachers, **You must become aware of the secrecy involved in gangs in order to hinder them because when you break down their secrecy, you break down the gangs**.

In Chicago, there are at least 135 different gangs. They consist of "Brothers" (although some people refer to them as "People") and "Folks." Gangs considered "Brothers" or "people" began with Jeff Fort, formerly of the El Rukns. "Brothers" wear their hats to the left; their colors are black and red. On the other side, "Folks," which started with Gregory Shell ("Shorty G") and are now run by the imprisoned Larry Hoover, wear their hats to the right; their colors are black and blue. In Chicago, the six-point stars represent "Folks"; five-point stars represent "Brothers." There are several factions of each gang that are discussed later in this manual. It is important to note that color schemes and choices among some gangs in Chicago are connected to gangs in other states.

For example, the "Bloods" in California wear black and red, which are the same colors worn by "Brothers" in Chicago. Also in California, the "Crips" wear black and blue, which is the same worn by "Folks" in Chicago. Therefore, it is logical to assume that each gang has several factions of their organization around the country.

Here is a partial list of these gangs:

"FOLKS"
(six-point star)
"Gangsters" (G)
"Gangster Disciples" (GD)
"Black Gangster Disciples" (BGD)
"Children of Satan" (COS)
"Spanish Gangsters" (SG)
"Black Disciples" (BD)
("Folks" or "Brothers" depending on who they follow)

"BROTHERS"
(five-point star)
"Latin Kings" (LK)
"Black Peace Stones" (BP)
"Black Peace Stone Nation" (BPSN)
"Vice Lords" (VL)
"Conservative Vice Lords" (CVL)
"Insane Vice Lords" (IVL)
"Maniac Four Corner Hustlers" (M4ch)
"Four Corner Hustlers" (4ch)
"Mickey Cobras" (MC)
"Mickey Cobra Nation" (MCN)

Some of the symbols used by these gangs are very sophisticated and are grouped differently. For "Brothers":

1. The Circle represents 360 degrees of knowledge that Black people once ruled the world before and will rule again.

2. Fire represents the Black nation's true knowledge of being suppressed and the inability to reach knowledge because of the heat created by the fire.

3. Darkness represents the Black majority, not minority, of the world.

4. The Crescent Moon represents the splitting of the Black nation into two parts: the East and West.

5. The Star represents the eye of Allah watching over His people.

6. The Pyramid signifies the mystery of the pyramids, which were constructed by Black people, with the three corners of the triangle representing wisdom, understanding and spiritual knowledge.

7. The Sun represents the rising of truth in the Black nation.

8. A Top Hat represents shelter.

9. A Cane represents the staff of strength.

10. Gloves represent purity.

With the gangs called "Folks," you might see young men standing around with their arms crossed, the right arm in front. Symbols for "Folks":

1. The Right Shoulder represents holding love for each other, the chairman and the entire organization.

2. The Head represents being in the frame of life, living and flourishing into something great.

3. The Left Shoulder represents holding loyalty above any negativity that may try to surface on the left side.

4. The Left Elbow represents the knowledge of obstacles and blocks against any form of opposition.

5. The Heel represents giving balance upon the path and wisdom down the road.

6. The Right Elbow crossing over the left represents a final point of locking them into understanding within the 360-degree circle of organization under the leadership of the chairman.

It takes a knowledgeable and intelligent person to develop a system as intricate as this. That is why it should be understood that some of these young people are highly intelligent. Also understand that these young people are very serious about their organizational structure, so much so that they will kill to maintain its secrecy. In fact, they have gone so far as to develop codes according to membership, which will be listed later in the book.

For instance, some children speak in code in front of their parents. Other people who are unaware of what they are talking about might think the children are playing. For example, if a child says "1-1-15," that would mean all's well; "4-24," death before dishonor; "9-12-25-23-21," I love you with understanding; "1-4-18," all due respect.

It must be understood that the gangs use **Masonic, satanic** and **religious** symbols as a guise to snare new members into their gangs. In most cases, gangs are not grouped by color or race, but instead, by the color of money. The gangs' main source of income is the distribution of drugs and it is this area of selling drugs that causes disputes and violence. Most of the victims are uninformed citizens.

In order to become a gang member a male or female must first go through **creation**—a three to four month probation period. During this period, the new member must prove himself to the leadership of the gang. A female can join a gang in several ways: 1) She may have sex with all of the male members of the gang; 2) She can draw blood from a rival gang; 3) She can pay her way into the gang or 4) She can be beaten into the gang which is considered a way of getting honors or high respect from the rest of the members. For males to join a gang, they must follow steps two through four. In some cases, the beating causes the would-be member's death.

While the new member is going through this **creation** period they must attend a **service,** which is a meeting usually held on a Friday. You can usually tell if there is a meeting **(service)** because there are two members on each corner of the block, looking out for rival gang members. The gang may have an open-air meeting where within minutes, you will see several male and female gang members gathering outside on a corner, in the park or in the middle of the block. At the open-air meeting, business will take place very fast such as the payment of dues and talking about new members coming into the gang. After the business has been conducted, they disburse quickly.

While the new member goes to the **service** meeting, they learn **acts** which are the rules and regulations of the gang they are joining. I don't mean the **Acts** that are in the Bible. The final part of the new member's initiation is the **blessing**. The **blessing** is when you are blessed and sworn in by oath, making you a full-fledged member of the gang.

Just because a person wears black and blue or black and red does not make him/her a gang member. Gang members will show and let you know they are gang members by the use of certain signs, because they are proud to be gang members. Like most people, they want to be part of an organization. Unfortunately, the organization they are a part of is one that deals in criminal activities. Gang membership, in some cases, comes about because of a lack of attention, guidance, understanding, and a feeling of unity at school and/or home. All gang members consider the other members as their family and, sometimes, more important than blood family.

It has been said peer pressure is the main reason youth join gangs, but a lot more is actually involved. There are different reasons for different members. Some want the attention. Some are bored. Only the individual can say what made him/her join a gang. The only way to ensure that a child is not a gang member would be to observe them with a surveillance camera 24 hours a day. But today's young people are so resourceful, they would turn the camera off so you couldn't see what they were doing.

Rank is attained by the level of knowledge regarding gang operations and the amount of money paid into the "**nation**," which is the name of the gang to which a person belongs. Once a person joins a gang, the only way he/she can get out is to drop his/her flag (request permission to become inactive), and depending on how high a rank he/she has attained within the gang, it is possible that the member would have to leave the city. Different gangs have territories, which they call a **set**, and only interact within their own areas or set. Within Chicago, I have never heard of a Caucasian gang fighting an African American gang, nor a gang from 103rd and Avenue L going down to 43rd and King Drive and shooting some African Americans. The fighting that occurs is not about race but about the locations of distribution of drugs and money.

I ask young gang members: When a gang member is shot, does the gang pay the doctor's bill? When a gang member is hit in the eye, does the gang buy that person eyeglasses or contact lenses, if needed? When a gang member is struck in the mouth, does the gang pay the dental bills? If the gang member needs to have a tooth replaced, capped, a partial or braces, does the gang pay for it? Does the gang provide all of the gang members with a defense attorney when they are arrested? Does the gang pay medical bills for the member who was shot and hospitalized? Does the gang have a retirement plan?

When the gang members turn 65 (if they live that long), will they receive $40,000 a year for the rest of their life? Does the gang have a burial policy for the members who are killed and a financial plan for the family that is left without a son or daughter? Does the gang teach young adults math, English, world history or, for that matter, their own history? What positive and constructive things does a gang do for the community at large? How many gang members does the gang train to become productive citizens that will be able to enter the mainstream with the ability to take proper care of themselves and a family? Does the gang teach members how to invest their money in the community business, stores, Johnson & Johnson, Ameritech or IBM? Does the gang reduce crime in the community? Does the gang protect the older citizens in the community from crimes? Does the gang educate young children in the community by taking them to the museums, parks, beaches, Art Institute, Sears Tower or the John Hancock building?

Does the gang tell members about the state of Illinois, the United States, Europe, Africa, Asia, France or Spain? I also ask how many gang members they know who have lived to be 25 or older. Their reply to all these questions are laughter and joking while shaking their heads no, stating that most of them die at an early age.

Most of the time when I speak to adults, I must remind them that they were young once because most adults think that the kids are born knowing everything. I asked those who own cars if they know when to change the oil or get a grease job? They know these things but when their children come into the house with new clothing or jewelry and say they borrowed it from a friend, they don't question it.

Today's young adults are very fast thinkers and you must keep up with them. Their language changes. Their clothing changes. If you don't pay attention, they will pass you by so fast that you won't know you were in the race. I'm 54 years old and remember when I was younger that crack was a split in the wall; pot was something you would cook in; tripping was accidentally falling; coke was something you would drink; grass was something that you would cut on weekends to make extra money and a drive-by was checking to see if the girl's mother was at home before you came over for a visit. Things have changed to such a large degree that we as adults must keep up in order to communicate with our young adults and keep them away from the street organizations.

Some common gang language includes:

1. Blocked - to be kicked out of the gang because of a "violation."

2. Violations - acts committed against the gang for which a member is disciplined.

3. "Make a move on" someone - to fight.

4. Perpetrate - to act like something that you are not.

5. False Flagging - saying that you belong to a particular gang when you do not.

6. Trick - to give information to the police about a person or group.

7. Digits - phone numbers.

8. Ducat - money.

9. Fronting - to put up a false pretense or air.

10. Tripping - to play around or joke.

In the organization called "Brothers," there are seven "acts" members must learn in order to participate in gang activities. In the Vice Lords, Latin Kings and El Rukns, a girl receives rank according to the amount of knowledge she possesses. For higher ranking, girls have to bring in other girls to become sisters. Queens are an exception to this rule.

The ranks are as follows:

1. Foot Soldiers, who observe what goes on around them.

2. Enforcers, who keep order at all services (meetings).

3. Head Enforcers, who rank over enforcers.

4. Enforcer Princess, who calls the meeting, location and collects the dues.

5. Governing Princess, supervisor of the Enforcer Princess.

6. Queen, who passes out literature and keeps all sisters in order.

7. Momma Stone, who holds all literature.

Boys also receive rank through the amount of knowledge they have.

The ranks include: Soldiers, Mufti, Head Mufti, General, Emir, Chief Emir, Prime Minister, Iman and Chief Iman.

GANGS, DRUGS AND VIOLENCE:
CHICAGO STYLE

When talking to elementary or high school students, the first thing that I do before starting any presentation, is ask them two questions, "Who is the most important person in the world?" and "Who's future are you?" Obviously, the answers to these questions are "I am the most important person in the world" and "I am my own future". I tell the students that I am not there to sweat them, but to give them a checkup from the neck up so they can have some backup when gang members try to hook them up. Now they know just what they are saying no to and not just guessing.

They also know that the information I give them will help make it easier to stay away from gang activity. That's what this book is all about—being able to communicate with the young adults—and not just talking around, over or through them but, in fact, talking with the young adults on an equal playing ground. I also let the young adults know they can make the correct choice in doing positive and constructive actions for a productive life.

When I speak to these young people, I let them know the seriousness of being in gangs. For example, about 350 people are admitted every day into the Cook County jail as inmates. One hundred people are released either on an "I-Bond," a personal recognizance bond, or a cash bond, which is 10 percent of the bond amount to secure release.

These are some of the serious things I talk to them about relating to being involved with gangs and criminal activity, along with the circumstances surrounding incarceration in the Cook County Jail. I let them know that jail is not a fun place to be, that when you go to jail, there is nothing in jail but other criminals. Just think about it, if you get sick, you go to a hospital where other sick people are. When you go to jail, there are only other criminals waiting for you.

A person going to jail in his late teens becomes vulnerable to those criminals who will do him bodily harm because it is difficult for prisoners to be watched 24 hours a day. Furthermore, even in jail, there are rules and regulations which must be obeyed. You have a room, a toilet, a washbowl, a bar of soap, toilet paper, a towel, a bed blanket, sheet, pillow and pillowcase, and you are told you must keep your area clean. You have commissary rights once a week where you are allowed to buy snacks and cigarettes. Most of the items an inmate wants to keep cold are tied in a plastic bag and kept in the toilet because of the cold water. Therefore, the toilet has to be kept very clean.

When you are sent to jail, there are only two things that you want to do: **do your time and stay alive**. In prison, the guards guard the prison and the inmates run the prisoners. In the "joint," as it is called, you cannot be watched by the guards 24 hours a day. In each section of the joint, there are tiers of floors that have head prisoners who call the shots when the guards are not around. You must follow orders here because if you don't, bad things might happen to you—including death. They have a saying in the joint: **either you can serve time or let time serve you**. That means you can do your time by trying to better yourself through education and staying clean from drugs and follow orders.

If you mind your business, you may just make it out of the joint alive. Things can happen to you very quickly in jail because if the guards don't get you, the gangs will. This is not a summer resort that you are going to, but jail, where you find all types of criminals—murderers, thieves, robbers, drug users, pimps and child abusers. In jail, you have no freedom at all. There are surprise inspections where the guards come into your jail cell at 4 a.m. and ask you to bend over so they can look up your behind while checking the cell for items that you should not have. They tell you when to eat, sleep, talk, walk and when you can go out on the exercise yard. If you don't want the food they serve, you don't eat. All of these things go for both sexes. A small thing like turning a TV channel can cost you your life if you did not get permission from the right prisoner.

You must constantly be on the lookout for trouble because being locked up in prison is meant to demoralize you. While you are in prison, you get paid less than minimum wage and, for all practical purposes, that's slave labor. Some people can go into jail, sentenced to a certain number of years, give the guards a hard time, talk back, start a fight or use profanity. Time for these prisoners will be extended by three months, or whatever the outcome of an in-house hearing determines. One might be originally sentenced to six months and wind up doing an extra three months or a year.

Statistics show that with a population of 8,000 men and women in the Cook County Jail, its population has increased by 60 percent from 1990 to 1991, double the 1989 rate of 30 percent. Currently, about 800 inmates are at home with electronic security bracelets on their wrists, which is called "house arrest." Seventy-five percent of all inmates in Cook County Jail are African American; 12 percent to 15 percent of the inmates are Caucasian and the remainder are Hispanic, Oriental, etc.

Of these inmates 95 percent are school dropouts, with 97 percent between the ages of 17 - 25, and serving as repeat offenders. Of those offenders who are African American, 95 percent have been previously arrested between 9 and 15 times. Seventy percent of all inmates are functional illiterates; some inmates can write, but cannot read, some can read but have no math skills and vice versa. To every young person who even thinks about joining a gang, I suggest they stay in school, which will decrease their chances of coming into contact with gangs and criminal activity, which could lead to incarceration. Since, statistically speaking, most crimes are committed between 8:00 a.m. and 3:00 p.m. while children are in school, being in school and getting an education during these hours will keep most youth out of the criminal justice system.

I ask children, "How many of you have had your home burglarized? Your VCR stolen? Your mother's jewelry or your father's watch taken? How many have had your Nintendo game taken? How many of you have had your little brother's TV taken out of his room?" I get quite a response when I bring it home to them, and most of the young people know the person(s) who burglarized their home. Research shows that 75 percent of most crimes committed in the community are committed by a person or persons who live within three to four blocks of the area. People in the community know who did it because the very person who burglarized someone's home will try to sell the stolen merchandise within the community. The people in the community will buy the merchandise, so they know who stole it. Most of the time it is gang members. Strange people do not come into communities and steal. In some cases, it is an organized gang effort. Seventy-five percent of all inmates are arrested for committing the same crime at least 60 percent of the time.

The same statistics and rules apply for females as well as males. Some inmates enter the Cook County Jail as "King of the Mountain" and leave as "Queen of the Sea." I get quite a bit of laughter out of that, simply because the kids understand what I am talking about. In other words, some inmates enter as a heterosexual and exit as a homosexual. When they say "OPP," they're talking about "other people's property"; a person can be passed around like a piece of candy. It is hard to be watched in a jail by guards who do not have closed circuit television to observe an inmate in a cell.

It is even harder for a person to be watched in a city like Chicago with a population of 2,800,000 and a police force of 12,000. Even with that number of officers in Chicago, at any one time there are fewer than 1,500 police officers actively patrolling the streets.

In the police department, there are watches or shifts. One watch starts at 7:00 a.m. and 8:00 a.m. and ends at 3:30 p.m. and 4:30 p.m. The next watch starts at 3:00 p.m. and 4:00 p.m. and ends at 11:30 p.m. and 12:30 a.m. Another watch starts at 11:00 p.m. and 12:00 a.m. ends at 7:30 a.m. and 8:30 a.m. On each watch, there might be 25 to 30 beat cars working and some of the beat cars are manned by two persons, some by one. That means about 1,500 officers are covering the city, which consists of 25 police districts. Not only are we outmanned at this time, we are also outgunned and most gang members know it.

However, the population of the Cook County Jail has been enlarged one hundredfold to incarcerate people participating in gang activity. The Audy Home, the local juvenile detention facility, has also been enlarged one hundredfold.

At one time, older people were participating in more gang activities, but that has now turned around. Younger people are now participating in gang activity, and gangs have become more sophisticated and more ruthless for financial reasons. Gangs are smarter and more organized.

The only problem is that the average citizen is not aware of gang activities. What we must do is inform teachers that any crime committed by a gang member--or anyone else, for that matter--within 1,000 feet of a school can cause that person to be arrested and charged with a felony, which is worse than a misdemeanor. Students can also help improve their school by anonymously reporting gang activity to their principal or any teacher. In turn, the principal/teacher can call the police department, who will take the proper action.

Most gangs are very sophisticated. They know logistics. They know marketing. They know research and development. They know security. They know how to hide their guns. They know finance and how to reinvest their money into drug sales. If given a chance, they could actually run the city. They have lookout people who keep them aware of when the police (**"Five-O"**) are coming. In some instances, they even have hand-held walkie-talkies and citizen band radios and listen to police calls. But, regardless of their skillfulness, I try to explain to them that all the know-how in the world, if used to commit crimes, will not keep them from getting arrested and going to jail.

The only people in jail are criminals and they will take physical advantage of you. Some females go to jail, become pregnant or are attacked and brutalized by fellow inmates or corrupt jail employees. Some people have even been killed in jail, because there are gangs there. In some instances, drugs have been found within the jail system itself. Even the toughest gang members have to fight for their protection while in the criminal justice system. Most adults believe that once their child enters high school, they no longer have to take care of him or her. This is unfortunate because once in high school, the young person often has to travel through new gang turfs ("sets") and environments. Consequently, the need for family support is even stronger than when the youth attended a neighborhood grammar school where they knew the different gang factions and dangers that existed there.

In high school, the child is more exposed and has a longer distance to travel. Most young people do not belong to gangs but they do know how to survive. They know how to wear their hats to the left or right in order to survive gang activity. Most young people know what, how, where and when to say what. In some instances, however, gang activity can become confusing. A child who is not a gang member might stand on a corner waiting for a bus and a gang member approaches and throws a sign of "Folks." But unknown to him, the gang member was faking him out and is a "Brother" who shoots the child who inadvertently gave the wrong gang sign.

In that particular circumstance, it is recommended to all young people that if they are not in a gang, they should not "false-flag." In other words, if someone approaches you and throws a gang sign, do not throw back any gang sign. Just say you are not a gang member and walk away. Think for yourself. Most of the attention these days is given to those young people who create havoc and are in gangs. It would behoove us as teachers and parents to reach out to those who are not involved in any gang activity or, for that matter, not causing any problems.

We should let them know that we appreciate them doing the correct things. We cannot ignore those who exhibit qualities like kindness.

GANGS, DRUGS AND VIOLENCE:
CHICAGO STYLE

Overlooking the good youth turns them into potential gang members. We must reach out to these youth and show them that we care. The gang members know how to reach out to these young people and give them the attention that is necessary for them to feel accepted.

All concerned adults—teachers, parents and citizens—must understand and do the same thing, but on a broader level. Parents, teachers, political leaders, state representatives, aldermen, ward committeemen and precinct captains should work collectively with the business community in our areas. Public schools should work with Catholic schools, the private school sector, YMCA, YWCA, the Boys and Girls Clubs, public libraries, community centers and the Chicago Park District. Everyone, including the police department, should work in a unified effort to give the youth some constructive activities to fill that void of boredom that they so often misuse.

Gang Names and Terminologies

| F - Folks ✡ | Colors are black and blue |
| B - Brothers ☆ | Colors are red and black |

Commonly used symbols for both gangs include: pitchforks, six-point stars, five-point stars, pyramids, hearts, canes, top hats, rabbit heads and gloves. Folks (F) are represented with six-point stars. Brothers (B) are represented with five-point stars.

Gang	Abbreviation
Gangsters (F) ✡	G
Gangster Disciple (F) ✡	G.D.
Black Disciple (F) ✡	B.D.
Black Gangster Disciple (F) ✡	B.G.D.
Latin Kings (B) ☆	L.K.
Black P Stone (B) ☆	B.P.S.

Black P Stone Nation (B) ☆   B.P.S.N.
Vice Lords (B) ☆   V.L.
Conservative Vice Lords (B) ☆   C.V.L.
Insane Vice Lords (B) ☆   I.V.L.
Maniac Four Corner Hustler (B) ☆   M4CH
Four Corner Hustlers (B) ☆   4CH
Mickey Cobra (B) ☆   M.C.
Mickey Cobra Nation (B) ☆   M.C.N.
Spanish Gangsters (F) ✡   S.G.
Children of Satan (F) ✡   C.O.S.

The following is a breakdown of some of the major gang organizations and some of their factions:

FOLKS

I. Gangster Disciples (G.D.) ✡

   A. Black Disciple Nation (B.D.N.)

   B. Black Gangster Disciples Nation (B.G.D.N.)

   C. Gangster Disciple Nation (G.D.N.)

   D. Spanish Gangsters (S.G.)

   E. Children of Satan (C.O.S.)

BROTHERS

II. Brothers of the Struggle (B.O.S.)

   A. Vice Lords

   B. Conservative Vice Lords (C.V.L.)

C.   Insane Vice Lords (I.V.L.)

D.   Four Corner Hustlers (4CH)

E.   El Rukns

F.   Black Stone (B.S.)

G.   Mickey Cobras (M.C.)

H.   Black P Stone (B.P.S.)

I.   Gangster Stones (G.S.)

J.   Latin Kings (L.K.)

K.   Royals

Rankings within the Vice Lords, Latin Kings and El Rukns (Brothers and Sisters)

El Rukns founder Jeff Fort, who is imprisoned, is the founder of all Brothers and Sisters. Boys and girls receive rank based on the amount of knowledge they have. Also to achieve higher ranking, they have to bring new males and females to become brothers and sisters, although Queens are an exception to this rule.

Girls
Foot Soldier   - observer of what is going on
Enforcer   - keeps order at all services
Head Enforcer   - keeps order at all services
Enforcing Princess   - calls meetings and law and collects dues
Governing Princess   - calls meetings and law and collects dues

| Queen | - passes out literature and keeps all sisters in order |
| Momma Stone | -there is only one and she knows all the literature |

Boys

Foot Soldier	follows Mufti orders
Mufti	keeps order at all meetings
Head Mufti	follows orders of General; collects dues
General	calls meetings and law
Emir	calls meetings and law
Chief Emir	makes laws of local set
Kaaba	teaches the younger brothers literature of the nation
Emon	holds (interprets) literature of the nation
Chief Emon	Dictates literature of the nation

Gang Terminology

Cancel	- kill
Cold brick/donuts	- Folks
Dick	- detective
Dis	- disrespecting someone
Dropped	- to be kicked out of a gang
Fly	- attractive girl or boy
Foul	- rotten
Fronting (fro'n)	- portraying a false image
"G"	- gangster or friend
Gad	- to shoot
Gaffle	- to fool
Gank	- to steal from

GANGS, DRUGS AND VIOLENCE: CHICAGO STYLE

Gang Terminology cont.

Hook	- Vice Lord
Hype	- drug addict
Kicking it (kick'n it)	- hanging out and having fun
Mac	- a flirt
Mark	- punk
Nappy dugout	- vagina
Outty 5000	- about to leave
Salty	- feeling stupid
Skeezer	- a girl who will have sex with anyone, anywhere, anytime
Serving	- selling drugs
Ya dig?	- do you understand?

FOLKS-colors are black and blue; symbols are pitchforks pointed up and six-point star; hats, jewelry and pants are worn to the right.

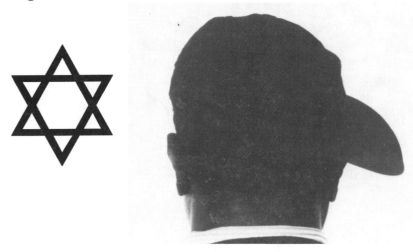

BROTHERS-colors are black and red; symbols are five-point star and a cane pointed up; hats, jewelry and pants are worn to the left.

GANGS, DRUGS AND VIOLENCE:
CHICAGO STYLE

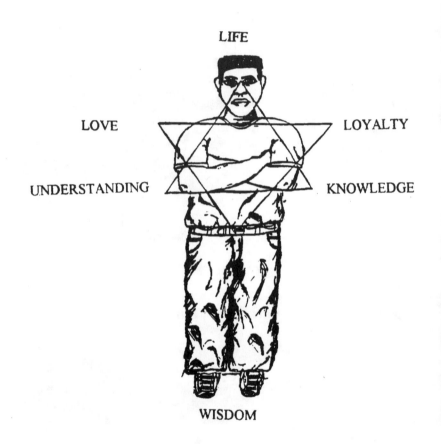

For an explanation of this pose, read the "Six-Point Stance of Folks" on the following page.

THE SIX-POINT STANCE OF FOLKS

1. The right shoulder represents Love.
The LOVE for each other, the chairman and the entire organization.

2. The head represents Life.
Being in the frame of LIFE, living and flourishing into something great.

3. The left shoulder represents Loyalty.
Holding LOYALTY above any negativity that may try to surface on the left side.

4. The right elbow represents Understanding.
Crossing over the left, serving as the final point of locking us into UNDERSTANDING within the 360-degree cycle (circle) of the organization under the leadership of the chairman.

5. The left elbow represents Knowledge.
Knowing the KNOWLEDGE around you and blocking against any form of opposition.

6. Heels of the feet represents Wisdom.
Giving us (members of the organization balance upon our path) and WISDOM down the road.

GANGS, DRUGS AND VIOLENCE: CHICAGO STYLE

FOLKS' POSE

Their symbol is a six-point star. The right arm symbolizes holding down the brothers--their opposition. Colors are black and blue.

THE SIX-POINT STAR OF FOLKS

1. The six-point star represents six principles of King David (dedicated to former Folks leader David Barksdale).

2. The pitchforks represent the nation's power in the struggle to overcome oppression.

3. The sword represents life and death within the nation and the struggle to survive at all costs.

4. The devil's horns represent nation's determination to overcome all obstacles.

5. The heart represents the love of the nation.

6. Seven and eight represents the year of the founding of the sons and daughters.

GANGS, DRUGS AND VIOLENCE:
CHICAGO STYLE

FOLKS' HAND SHAKE-Members shake hands with "pitchforks" pointed up. Colors are black and blue. Everything goes to the right.

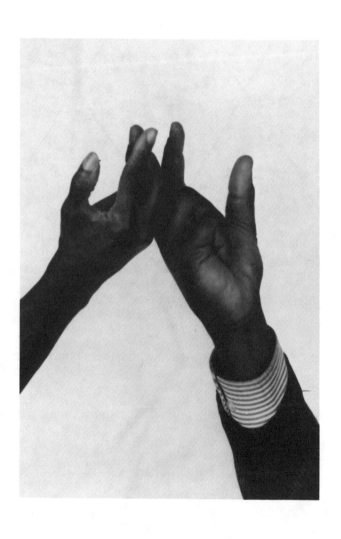

BROTHERS' POSE

Their symbol is a five-point star. The left arm symbolizes holding down folks--their opposition. Colors are black and red.

GANGS, DRUGS AND VIOLENCE:
CHICAGO STYLE

BROTHERS' HAND SHAKE-Members shake hands in a pyramid style. Colors are black and red. Everything to the left.

THE CONSERVATIVE VICE LORD'S INSIGNIA

1. The circle represents 360 degrees of knowledge that black people once ruled the world and will again rule the world.

2. Fire represents the black nation's true knowledge of being suppressed and its inability to reach knowledge because of the heat created by the fire.

3. Darkness represents the black majority, not minority, of the world.

4. The crescent moon represents the splitting of the Black nations into two parts, one of the west and one of the east.

5. The star represents the eye of Allah, watching over his people.

GANGS, DRUGS AND VIOLENCE: CHICAGO STYLE

Black Disciples (Folks)

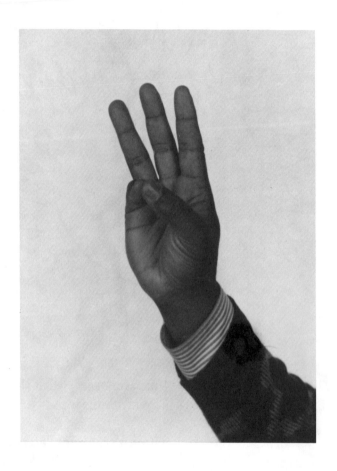

Six-point star ✡
Everything to the right
Colors are black and blue

Gangster Disciples (Folks)

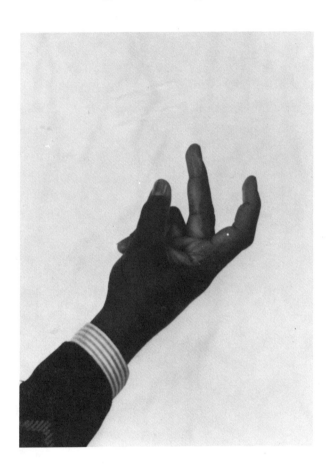

Six-point star ✡
Everything to the right
Colors are black and blue

Mickey Cobras (Brothers)

Five-point star ☆
Everything to the left
Colors are red and black

Black Peace Stones (Brothers)

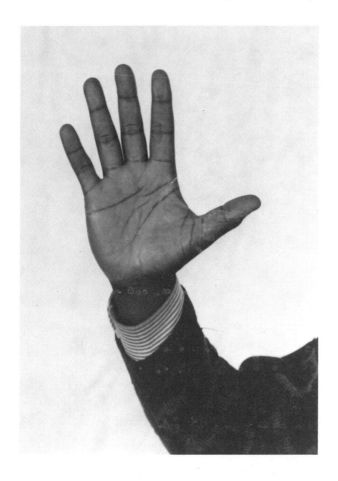

Five-point star
Everything to the left
Colors are red and black

GANGS, DRUGS AND VIOLENCE: CHICAGO STYLE

Four-Corner Hustlers (Brothers)

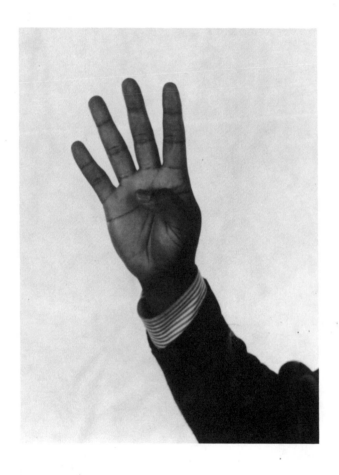

Five-point star
Everything to the left
Colors are red and black

Vice Lords (Brothers)

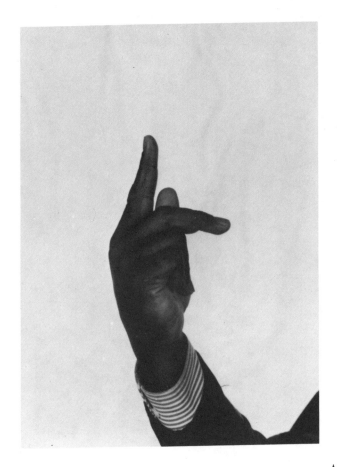

Five-point star
Everything to the left
Colors are red and black

GANGS, DRUGS AND VIOLENCE: CHICAGO STYLE

Latin Kings (Brothers)

Five-point star
Everything to the left
Colors are black and yellow/gold

All Mighty Latin King Nation (Brothers)

Five-point star ☆
Everything to the left
Colors are black and yellow/gold

GANGS, DRUGS AND VIOLENCE:
CHICAGO STYLE

White Power Skinheads

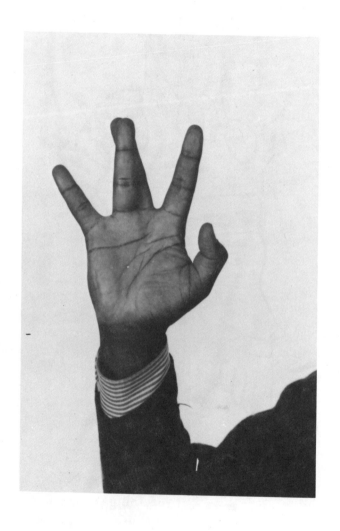

Caucasians and African Americans Against Skinheads (Antis)

In this photo, "C.V.L.N." means Conservative Vice Lord Nation (although the abbreviation "CVL" is more commonly seen). "C-Note" is the pseudonym for one of the members of the C.V.L.N. "Riverside" is the name of a territory occupied by the C.V.L.N. "Hook Killer" is how the Vice Lords are referred to as a sign of disrespect. The upside down triangle with a split and upside down pyramid represents the Vice Lords. The pitchfork pointing downward is a sign of disrespect to the Gangster Disciples, a rival gang of the Conservative Vice Lords. The letter K placed after "C.V.L.N." was done by a rival gang member as a sign of disrespect.

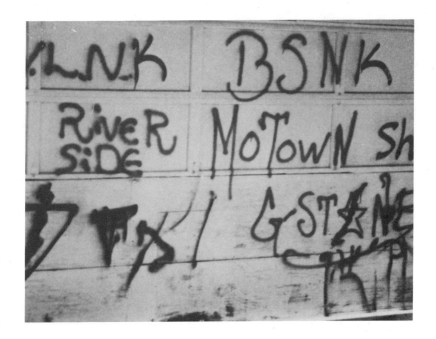

In this photo, "BSNK" means "Black Stone Nation Killer," which is disrespectful to the Black P Stone Nation. "Motown" is a territory occupied by Black Stones. "G-Stone" means "Gangster Stone," the name of a gang associated with Black Stones and Vice Lords. The five-point star, a symbol representing all Brothers, is split as a sign of disrespect to the Brothers.

Here are symbols representing the Black Disciples Nation, which is sometimes abbreviated "BDN." "Nell D" (the D refers to the BDN), "Tino" and "Do Doo" are nicknames of gang members. "BPSK" means Black P Stone Killer and is a form of disrespect to that gang.

The letters "BDN," written between two horizontal lines, appear as "III." This symbol is called a "trey" and represents the BDN. The numbers 2-4 represent the second and fourth letters in the alphabet. "Brandi" is the name of one of the members of this gang.

GANGS, DRUGS AND VIOLENCE:
CHICAGO STYLE

In this picture, the letters "BD" stand for Black Disciples, and "BPSK" stands for Black Peace Stone Killer, which is a branch of the nation called "Folks." "BPSK" shows disrespect to the gang known as the Black Peace Stones.

The cracked five-point star in this photo shows disrespect to the
Brothers. "Nell D" is the name of one of the members of the gang.
"12-3" means 123rd Street. Street names often are abbreviated.
"12-3" is pronounced "twelve trey."

The symbols above represent the Gangster Disciples, which is often abbreviated G.D. or "G" (meaning "gangster"). GDs use a six-point star, better known as the star of David, and pitchforks, both of which are seen here, to represent themselves. The star represents love, life, loyalty, knowledge, wisdom and understanding. The pitchfork represents the Gangster Disciple Nation's power to overcome oppression.

Here are more marks from the GDs, including the letter D with a pitchfork protruding from the top. It stands for "Disciple," although it is also used by the Black Disciples. The pitchfork makes it a representation of the Gangster Disciples. "11-9 MB" is the name of a "set" (boundaries of the gang) of the GDs. "11-9" is 119th Street, and "MB" is an abbreviation for "May Berry." "11-9" and "MB" are used to state the name of the set.

The Maniac Four-Corner Hustlers represent themselves with the
number four that is drawn with a longer horizontal axis that connects
the vertical and slanted lines of the four. An M, which stands for
"maniac," is placed on top of the number. Above the horizontal
line is the letter C ("corner") , and   beneath the line is an
H (" Hustlers"). The pitchfork represents the Gangster Disciples
and is pointed upside down because the M4CH gang is showing
disrespect to the Gangster Disciples.

"RIP J-BABY" is used to recognize the death of a member of M4CH gang. "J-BABY" is a pseudonym for a member of the gang. The letter A in "J-BABY" is upside down to symbolize an upside down pyramid, which is a sign of disrespect to the Black P Stone gang.

In this picture, the letters "BG" are an abbreviation for the Black Gangsters. "7-4" represents the seventh and fourth letters of the alphabet, and is a code used to represent the abbreviated name of the Gangster Disciples: G(7) D(4). The pitchfork also represents the Gangster Disciples.

This picture shows a cracked five-point star with an upside down cane. The star, a symbol used by Brothers to represent themselves, is a sign of disrespect to the Brothers when cracked. The cane, a symbol used by Vice Lords to represent themselves, is a sign of disrespect when turned upside down.

The photo above depicts the letters and abbreviations G, GD and BPS. BPS stands for Black P Stone, which is a branch of the organization known as Brothers. The letter G inside of the six-point star, with a pitchfork protruding from its top, is a reference to the Gangster Disciples (GD).

The letters seen in the photo above are abbreviations for the Black Gangster Disciples, which should not be confused with the Gangster Disciples. The Black Gangster Disciples also use the six-point star and pitchfork to represent themselves. This is another branch of the gang known as Folks.

This photo shows numerous symbols representing a Hispanic gang known as the Latin Kings whose symbols include a five-point crown and a drawing of a king wearing a crown. The letters "LKN" stand for Latin King Nation. Often the word King is seen alone, but also represents the gang. Latin Kings are also in the nation called Brothers, which explains the upside down pitchfork, a sign of disrespect to the Folks, the Brothers enemy.

The Latin Kings are foes of the Gangster Disciples, which is why the pitchfork is shown upside down. Many Latin Kings are exceptional artists. Often, their signs look more like art than gang graffiti.

The symbols in this picture represent the Four-Corner Hustlers (M4CH) and the Gangster Disciples (GD). The pitchfork protruding from the top of the D is a symbol for Gangster Disciples. "BPSK" means Black P Stone Killer, a sign of disrespect to the Black P Stone gang. "11-9" and "MB" stand for "May Berry".

The upside down M4CH with a K at the end shows disrespect to the Four-Corner Hustlers gang.

This photo shows the letters G and D for Gangster Disciples, the name of a branch of Folks. "G" means Gangster, and is a commonly used abbreviation for GD. The letter G is usually used after a person's name (i.e. "Freddy G.").

GANG CODES

1.	A	Allah, as, all
2.	B	Be, Born, Brother, Black
3.	C	See, Cobra, Club
4.	D	Divine, Disciples, Daughters, Death, Dishonor
5.	E	Equity
6.	F	Father, Folks
7.	G	God, Gangsters
8.	H	He, Her, Hoover
9.	I	Islam
10.	J	Justice
11.	K	Kingdom, Knowledge
12.	L	Love, Life, Loyalty, Leave
13.	M	Master, Much
14.	N	Nation
15.	O	One
16.	P	Power, People, Pure, Plenty

GANGS, DRUGS AND VIOLENCE: CHICAGO STYLE

17.	Q	Quality
18.	R	Right, Righteous, Ruler, Respect
19.	S	Self, Savior, Sons, Stand, Struggle, Star
20.	T	True, Truth, To, The, Think
21.	U	Unity, Understanding, Universe
22.	V	Victory
23.	W	Wisdom, With, We, Win
24.	X	
25.	Y	Why, You
26.	Z	Zig, Zag

Note: Members of all the gangs must maintain a code of silence when not in a place of privacy.

DD	- Drug dealer	6	- White
77	- Smoke	S.O.P.	- Standard operating procedure
88	- Girl		
66	- Tac	9-1	- Kill
55	- Drink	E7	- Meeting
K-9	- Police	SR	- Status report
4	- Female	PC	- Present location
		CIT	- Check in time

Chapter 2
DRUGS

Drugs are sold by gang members for one purpose, and one purpose only, but that purpose is twofold: To make money from the buyer and to get the buyer addicted to the drug the gang sells. The only drug that any person should take is the drug that is prescribed to him/her by a qualified physician, and that prescription should be taken to a certified pharmacist. All drugs prescribed by doctors are designated for a certain person's age, weight, sex, etc., so no one, not even relatives, should take drugs prescribed for anyone other than themselves.

Illegal drugs on the street are made in a clandestine way, and although most people do not realize it, drugs are ethnic to a great degree. For example, in Hispanic neighborhoods, the common drugs are cocaine, heroin and marijuana. The drugs commonly used in Caucasian communities are LSD, PCP, other hallucinogenic drugs and, in some cases, glue by placing it on a rag, dropping it into a paper bag and inhaling. Glue-sniffing makes a person quite intoxicated, causes loss of hair, formation of bumps around the nostrils, receding hairlines and pale skin.

Another popular inhalant in the Caucasian community is a chemical called tauline - street name "pollywog" - which is engine cleaner that is inhaled in the same manner as glue. This chemical literally eats your brain and causes disorientation and impaired coordination. In the African American community, the drugs commonly used are marijuana , cocaine (powder and "crack") and ready rock. A motorcycle gang called Hell's Angels monopolizes the distribution of a drug called "crank," which is made from three different man-made liquid chemicals. And Native Americans use a drug called "peyote," which is made from several plants and herbs. Many people do not realize that most drugs sold by so-called instant drug factory makers are mixed with several different chemicals to enhance the high and thereby entice the buyer to return to that particular seller. For instance, cocaine is mixed with quinine, milk, sugar and Darvon.

Cocaine is usually, as is referred to on the street, "stepped on" at least seven times before it is sold. For buyers to make more money off of the drugs they purchase, milk sugar is added to stretch the quantity.

A pure shot or piece of cocaine would kill the average American, so buyers "knock down" the purity of cocaine by adding on several other drugs like Darvon (a pain killer); Quinine (originally used for malaria and yellow fever it stimulates certain anatomical molecular structures and gives the person a feeling of being high); Formaldehyde (an embalming fluid); and Ether (an anesthetic that is highly concentrated and explosive). "Tac," a man-made chemical used as an tranquilizer, is added to marijuana. Cocaine is sometimes used with tac and is called "tac caine."

All drugs sold on the street break down the body's molecular structure and destroy white corpuscles, thereby lowering the immune system and leaving users susceptible to disease. A person might consider themselves enjoyably high and hallucinating, but they are killing themselves at the same time by not eating or keeping clean, and sharing needles, which spreads AIDS and other diseases.

Currently, there is a rebirth of a previously abused drug called "Ice " for its resemblance to ice crystals. Chiang Kai-Shek, a general in Upper Mongolia, had this synthetic drug made and given to his troops because it caused them to believe themselves to be "supermen." When the Japanese invaded China and Mongolia, they discovered and adopted the use of the drug. It was then passed on to Korea, Hawaii, and later to Southern California.

Abuse of the drug is now spreading across the United States. "Ice" is considered extremely dangerous because of the economy involved in its use. One bag, which costs approximately $3, will get the user "bombed out of his/her skull" for at least seven days. Continuous use of "Ice" will kill.

"Ice" has a heavy downside. A person coming down off of a five-day binge becomes quite paranoid, thinks people are following them and becomes very scared and suicidal. This paranoia reaches a point where "Ice" users become dangerous to themselves and others. "Ice" is very cheap, but its low cost might limit the time it is abused in the United States because dealers cannot make large sums of money selling drugs for $3 per bag. However, to experience the same level of high as the first usage, "Ice" users must spend twice the amount of money each time they buy .

Anyone would be well advised not to take any drug unless it's prescribed by his or her doctor. Some drugs can be ingested through the pores of the skin and activated by body chemicals, causing hallucinations. Most people do not realize that a drug may not immediately activate after being consumed. Therefore, a person who only "tries" a drug might find themselves six months later having a delayed drug reaction that could resemble an epileptic seizure and possibly cause a coma.

In most cases involving known users of marijuana, cocaine, heroin, crack or LSD, milk can "bring them down" as it decreases the flow of molecular-changing chemicals through the body. However, under no circumstances would milk be recommended for persons who have taken acid because milk and acid combined may cause damage to the body while being regurgitated.

Male and female gang members can prey on other young individuals simply because they know how to contact and reach young minds: mainly by giving them attention, making them feel important and like they belong to a special group (family). Females can carry drugs, money and weapons and sometimes are not searched because of a lack of female police officers on the streets at the time. Women tend to be less conspicuous and keep lower profiles, but are very active in the drug trade. Young females should understand that drugs are very detrimental to their lifestyles.

For example, according to *Reader's Digest,* crack cocaine has terrible effects on an unborn fetus because it causes the blood vessels in the placenta to constrict, creating a shortage and slower receipt rate of nutrients to the fetus. Placenta nutrients first go to the brain, then organs, bones, and finally fat cells. Constriction of blood vessels can cause the infant to have a head 20 percent smaller than normal, as well as dry, cracked skin that resembles a book cover.

Nationwide, perhaps hundreds of thousands of drug-exposed infants are born each year. It costs the government $15 billion a year to prepare drug-babies for entry into kindergarten. At one time in certain parts of the country, laws were introduced to charge females with contributing to the delinquency of a minor for giving the unborn fetus illegal drugs without consent. However, this was found to be unsatisfactory because many young pregnant women became afraid and would not seek prenatal care, causing an even greater problem among unwed mothers.

In some states, the practice was soon abolished. It was found that 71 percent of crack mothers had poor or no prenatal care versus 26 percent of non-users in the same low-income neighborhood. Crack children score lower on standardized development tests because of their mother's use of crack. Because of the smallness of the brain and a disrupted growth period, these children are slow learners. The percentage of crack babies also born with AIDS is not known, but considered high. To supply their habits, women on crack will have sex with anyone, creating the possibility of contracting this disease. Due to these mothers' promiscuity, not only are some children being born addicted to drugs and with AIDS, but also afflicted with venereal diseases. Crack babies cry uncontrollably; their limbs jerk constantly. Their hands fly to the sides of their heads and their eyes freeze wide open as though they're startled and terrified.

Drug addiction for females is becoming a major problem in the United States and throughout the world. Even countries such as Russia, with its new-found freedom, have discovered drug addiction and gangs. Some children have become so addicted, they have stolen from their parents as well as other people and, in some cases, females and males have prostituted themselves for money to buy drugs. Gang members are well aware of the fact that most young people will try anything just to be a part of a group.

If being a part of the group means buying drugs from them in order to be allowed to "hang out" with and be a part of the group, young people should realize that the group is not interested in their well being. Drugs are becoming more dangerous because people think it is a lucrative business. The average dealer stays in existence anywhere from six to nine months. If they are lucky, and stay alive, they're in the business for one year, because drug dealers become very paranoid. Dealers can be stopped by being arrested by the police and with the help of good citizens who provide information on drug sales in their communities.

Because of drugs, unknown persons come into the community and disrupt the normal flow of life, causing a high rate of burglaries, robberies and homicides. Anyone addicted will do anything to obtain drugs. Heroin and cocaine are usually sold in aluminum foil packets, wrapped several different times to resemble miniature envelopes. Marijuana is usually sold in a small brown envelope, but in some instances, criminals have become innovative and used Kool Aid packets to package the drug.

Statistically speaking, most people involved in incidents are unaware of what is going on around them. Drug sales are evident in areas where there is unusually heavy traffic around a particular corner where persons are standing in and around a particular house.

While working in the third district one day in a beat car, my partner and I got a call over the radio to go to a location where a man was selling marijuana out of his apartment. We went to the location, went up to the door and rang the bell. A male voice on the other side of the door asked "Who is it?" At that point, the female officer who was my partner started to say "Police," but I told her to just give her name, which she did. The man opened the door and you can imagine the look on his face when he saw two police officers in full uniform.

As he opened the door, I looked behind him and saw a small table with a cigar box that contained crushed green plants (marijuana). I immediately told him he was under arrest for possession of marijuana and stepped inside the apartment to advise him of his rights by law. I went on to say I would be calling the dogs in to search the apartment for more drugs. The arrestee stated that he didn't have any more drugs in the apartment. I then asked the offender if he had any weapons in the apartment.

He explained that he did have a gun for his protection and showed us where it was located. We were in the bedroom, removing the gun from the dresser drawer, when I detected a very strong odor of marijuana and began to search the closet and found several shopping bags full of drugs, then in the kitchen I found more drugs. There were still more drugs under the bed as well as in another room. The apartment search also yielded white powder, a suspected control substance and several hundred pounds of marijuana which we transported into the district station along with the arrestee for processing.

This arrest was made because we were informed by some citizen who saw what was going on and called the police. It is a known fact that the police are only as good as the citizens who report the crimes to the police. As a police officer, I know that most people do not commit crimes in front of the police and that when a crime is committed, someone in the community does see what happens, they just do not want to get involved until it's too late or until it happens to them.

Dealers can be stopped by being arrested by the police and with the help of good citizens who provide information on drug sales in their communities.

Several hundred pounds of marijuana were confiscated after the drug bust. Pictured here are some bags of the drug.

Drug Recognition

Tranquilizers, Alcohol and Barbiturates

EYES	Horizontal Nystagmus (Tranquilizers = No Nystagmus) Impaired, Smooth Pursuit Near Normal Pupils
	(Methaqualone = Dilated Pupils (>6.5 mm) Slow Pupillary Reaction Strabismus
VITAL SIGNS	Respiratory Depression Decreased Pulse Rate (>60 beats per minute)
OTHER EFFECTS	Drunken Behavior (No Odor) Thick, Slurred Speech Disorientation Gait Ataxia Impaired Coordination and Balance Drowsiness Knee Tremors (Methaqualone) Impaired, Divided Attention
OVERDOSE	Shallow Respirations Cold, Clammy Skin Dilated Pupils Weak, Rapid Pulse Coma/Death

DURATION	1- 16 hours	Barbiturates
	4 - 8 hours	Methaqualone
	4 - 8 hours	Tranquilizers
	5 - 8 hours	Chloral Hydrate

ADMINISTRATION	Oral
	Injected

Drug Recognition: Diet Pills, Cocaine, Crack and "Ice"

EYES	No Nystagmus
	Dilated Pupils (<6.5mm)

VITAL SIGNS	Increased Alertness
	Extremity and body tremors
	Restless
	Anxious
	Talkative, Rapid and Rambling Speech
	Excitation
	Euphoria (Pleasurable sensations)
	Insomnia
	Hyperflexia (Exaggerated reflexes)
	Bruxism
	Dry Mouth
	Increased Visual Acuity
	Impaired Coordination and Balance
	Gait Ataxia
	Red & Irritated Nasal Area
	(Cocaine)
	Evidence of malnutrition

OVERDOSE	Agitation
	Elevated Body Temperature

Hallucinations
Convulsions
Cardiovascular Collapse
Respiratory Failure
Death

DURATION	Amphetamines	(oral)
	30 - 20 minutes	Onset
	4 - 8 hours	Wired
	Cocaine	(Snorted)
	15 - 30 seconds	Onset
	5 - 15 minutes	Peak
	15 - 20 minutes	Wired
	60 - 90 minutes	Normal

ADMINISTRATION   Oral, Snorted, Injected, Smoked (Crack or
Free Basing)

Drug Recognition

Hallucinogens: LSD, PCP, Peyote and Psilocybin

EYES   No Nystagmus
                                   Dilated Pupils (<6.5mm)

VITAL SIGNS   Increased Pulse rate (<100BPM)
                                   Hypertension
                                   Elevated Body Temperature

OTHER EFFECTS   Memory Loss
                                   Change in Perception of
                                   Self (Hypersensitive)

Paranoia (LSD)
Flashbacks
Mood Changes (Mescaline)
Facial Flushing
Sweating
Tearing
Piloerection (LSD)
Decreased Muscular Coordination
Muscle Twitching
Yawning
Gait Ataxia
Impaired Time and Depth Perception
Dizziness
Hallucinations
Blurred Vision
Headaches
Nausea
Impaired Hearing
Difficulty With Speech
Fine Tremor in Fingers and Hands
Impaired, Divided Attention

OVERDOSE   Longer, More Intensive Trips
                  Psychosis
                  Possible death

DURATION   Variable

ADMINISTRATION   Oral, Infected, Snorted

Drug Recognition

Inhalants: White Out brand correction fluid, Glue, Toluene, Pollywog, Pam brand vegetable oil, Engine Cleaner, etc.

EYES	Nystagmus
VITAL SIGNS	Decreased Pulse rate (<60 BPM) Hypertension
OTHER EFFECTS	Impaired Coordination and Balance Disorientation or Confusion Thick, Slurred Speech Gait Ataxia Odor of Substance Used Impaired, Divided Attention
OVERDOSE	Coma Death
DURATION	6 - 8 hours
ADMINISTRATION	Inhaled

The Effect of Crack Cocaine on Babies

*   Cocaine used by the mother causes the placental blood vessels to constrict (tighten).

*   When blood vessels tighten, there is a shortage of food to the embryo. The shortage of food in the embryo causes the most important parts of the fetus to be fed first. The brain cells are fed and then the organs and bones. Finally, the fat cells are fed. This order of feeding through the tightened blood vessels causes the skin to crack and feel dry, like the leather cover of a book. The slower feeding causes the infant's head to become 20 percent smaller than normal.

*   Nationwide, hundreds of thousands of drug-exposed infants are born each year.

*   It costs the government $15 billion a year to prepare drug babies for entry into kindergarten.

*   Seventy-one percent of crack mothers had poor or no parental care compared to 26 percent of non-users in the same low-income neighborhoods.

*   Due to mothers' use of crack, their children invariably score lower in standardized developmental tests.

*   At birth, most crack babies weigh less than normal babies.

*   Because many crack cocaine-addicted mothers have traded sex for the drug and had multiple sex partners, their children also are born addicted.

Chapter 3
VIOLENCE

Most young gang members are told by older members that it is a badge of honor to be shot or cut. These younger members are not well-informed about the realities of being injured by guns or knives. They have never been told that when they are taken to the emergency room for treatment, the doctors begin by cutting off their clothing with electrical scissors, within seconds, and putting needles in their arms, into their chest.

Doctors sometimes insert a rubber tube directly into the victim's chest after administering a local anesthetic. They want to keep the patient awake so that he will stay alert and not slip into shock. Most of the doctor's time is spent doing exploratory surgery trying to repair the damage caused by the gunshot or stabbing. In some cases, veins from the patient's leg is removed and used to aid circulation to the kidney, liver, small intestines and other vital organs. When a bullet enters the body, it fragments and pulverizes bones, destroys blood vessels, ligaments, cartilage and muscle.

These young, uninformed members are not told that the smaller the caliber of bullet, the farther it will travel through the body and the more damage it will cause. They also don't know the larger caliber of bullet removes larger sections of the body. A 22-caliber bullet can travel through the body which can damage several parts of the body simultaneously. A 38-caliber bullet can blow your hand off. A 45-caliber can remove your arm up to the elbow, while a shotgun can remove your arm altogether. Gang members aren't told that 85% of those injured do not die but, in fact, live with their injuries. In many cases, these young adults are left without eyes, legs, arms or even sexual organs.

I warn young people that they will not grow another limb once it's been shot off. That leg or arm can be replaced only with an artificial device. A bullet may enter the left shoulder, travel through the lungs, across to the right side of the body, hit a bone, ricochet down past the liver, into the intestines and cause serious damage that might leave a person physically handicapped for the rest of his or her life.

In my line of work, I have seen a large range of these often grotesque injuries. Some of these include people with their legs and arms blown off or parts of their face shot away by a shotgun to the extent where they can no longer go out in public and be seen without wearing a scarf wrapped around their face and tied at the neck. Children 11-and 12-years old are injured to the point where they must wear pacemakers to regulate their heartbeat. Girls have had their breasts blown away and their sex organs so damaged that they are unable to give birth.

As a result of gunshot wounds, youths' bodies no longer function normally, causing them to make weekly or even monthly visits to the hospital. While at home, they live with the discomfort of having a dialysis machine connected to their bodies to clean their blood. I have even seen youth who have been stabbed or lacerated with knives, glass or ice picks, and the lacerations have torn the tissue and ligaments. They are left permanently disfigured. Their hands can no longer grasp objects. They are confined to wheelchairs.

The arteries have been cut so severely that they cannot be sewed back together. Muscles have been torn and can no longer be repaired. The injuries inflicted by knives and other dangerous weapons leaves a person psychologically traumatized, often rendering them unable to function in society as a normal person.

The family of the injured youth is also traumatized. Family members must change their behavior. When they are around the wounded person, they must choose their words carefully and decide how to communicate around the wounded family member. Hours of intense therapy have to be provided by a trained specialist who would come into the home to help that youth and instruct their parents and siblings on how to care for the victim.

Youth who were once mobile become so psychologically affected by the injury they withdraw from society. If they are a minority, they become a hidden minority within a minority. They refuse to be seen by other people who make disparaging remarks and derogatory comments about their appearance and what caused their injuries. It is unfortunate, but most youth do not face the reality of the injury. They look at it as a joke. But realistically, it could happen to anyone, any time, any place. Usually the injured youth is not a participant in any criminal activity, or he/she fails to believe that there is criminal activity and tries to hide from the fact. On the other hand, criminals who participate in illegal activity know who their enemies are (rival gangs and other drug dealers). Consequently, when another rival comes around, the criminals who are involved in drug dealing or other illegal acts duck and hide while the average citizen who is not well-informed often suffers a violent injury.

A person should, under all circumstances, be observant and watchful at all times, especially when walking down the street. Make sure you look behind yourself from time to time. When you get ready to enter your home, have your key in hand; if possible, call someone before you come home to let him or her know you are on your way.

If someone is dropping you off, have that person stay and wait to make sure you get in safe. If you are parking your car, look around before you get out and check to see who is coming, who is walking toward you and determine whether or not you know them.

If you see someone who is suspicious, continue on your way and have the police come back with you. An ounce of caution is worth a pound of cure. The nature of crime is such now that it can happen to anyone. Most females are very nonchalant when carrying a purse. It is the simplicity of crime that creates violence.

A female should never carry valuables like keys, money, or identification in a large purse. If you do carry valuables in a purse when walking down the street, place it in front of you, not hanging off your side. To do the latter is to advertise to some youngster to snatch your purse or fight with you over the bag. If they grab it, let them have it. If you resist, he might turn around and hurt you.

Even veteran police officers can become lax. The most dangerous time in my life was when I made an undercover purchase of cocaine. Before the buy, we wrote down the numbers on the bills and the amount of the money that would be used to buy the drugs. We then made a list of personnel that would be at the location of the buy. Also, we made a description of the person that we would buy the drugs from: height, weight, complexion, age, and, sometimes, his name and address with social security number, arrest record, etc.

After arriving at the location of the buy and waiting about five minutes, the dealer showed up. I had just given him the money for the coke. He put the money in his pocket after giving me the drug. A black male then came around the corner. He then pointed at me and shouted I was a pig. At that point, the dealer I had just paid turned and gave the money to a female who was standing by. She started running north from the location.

The offender who sold me the drugs took off in the other direction. He ran around the corner into a tavern with me close behind in hot pursuit, my weapon drawn. After entering the tavern, the offender turned and pointed a snub nose 38 revolver at me. I looked him in the face with my weapon pointed at him and said, "Drop your gun or I'll shoot." The offender looked at me, shook his head and dropped the 38 to the floor. I recovered the weapon, advised the offender of his rights and transported him to the district station for booking. While at the station, the rest of the crew came in with the woman who tried to run with the money and the man who blew my cover. These two were charged with obstruction of the police in the performance of his duty. I had given the gun to one of the crew while I was taking inventory of the drugs and during all the action, had forgotten to unload the weapon.

The crew person was about to unload the 38 snub nose the offender pointed at me and had just opened the chamber when he noticed the bullet behind the hammer was scored. I then understood why the drug dealer shook his head before dropping the gun as I told him. He had pulled the trigger, but the gun did not fire. That's why the back of the bullet was scored. At that moment, I realized I could have been killed, if not seriously injured. I began to break out in a cold sweat and started to shaking to such a degree I had to go run some cold water on my face and head to get myself under control.

Any police officer who says he is not scared out on the streets is a fool and a big liar because if he isn't scared, he will become lax. I know to this day the only reason I am here is by the grace of God in making that gun misfire.

Cook County Jail . . . At A Glance

1. Each day, 350 people are admitted into Cook County Jail. Because of a lack of space, 100 people are released from Cook County Jail each day on an "I Bond" (personal recognizance).

2. There are 8,000 inmates in Cook County Jail. The number of County Jail inmates is up 30 percent, which is the rate of the nation's population growth from 1989-90.

3. More than 800 inmates are at home with electronic security bracelets on their wrist or ankle and are monitored by the Cook County Sheriff's Department.

4. Seventy-five percent of the inmates in the County Jail are African Americans. The remaining inmates are Hispanic, Oriental, etc.

5. Ninety-five percent of all inmates are school dropouts. Seventy percent of all inmates are functionally illiterate.

6. Ninety-seven percent of the inmates are between the age of 17 and 25 and most are repeat offenders.

7. Ninety-five percent of the repeat offenders are African Americans and have been previously arrested nine to 15 times. Ninety percent of the people in Cook County were arrested on drug-related charges.

8. There are several gang factions in the Cook County Jail, including BGDN, Vice Lords, Royals, Disciples, etc.

9. Like the male inmates, females in the Cook County Jail have been brutalized and in some cases have become pregnant.

Facts You Should Know About
Crime and Criminal Justice

The U.S. Justice Department estimates that, nationwide, 10,000 guns are brought into public schools each day.

Less than 68 percent of all Americans believe that stricter gun control would not have any impact on violent crimes.

Americans have 67 million handguns in their homes. There are 200 million guns in circulation. Forty-eight percent of Americans have some type of gun in their homes.

The estimated total cost of firearm injuries to the U.S. economy is $14 million. The annual hospital cost for treating firearm injuries is $1 billion.

Seventy percent of Americans favor stricter gun control laws.

Seventy-four percent of Americans favor a law that would make it illegal for any private citizen to own a handgun for any purpose.

Between 1980-1990, the national arrest rate of young black males charged with weapons offenses jumped 102 percent.

Facts You Should Know About
Crime and Criminal Justice

Across the country, between 1980-1990, the murder rate of young males soared by 145 percent and aggravated assault by 89 percent.

During 1993, in Chicago, 73 African Americans under the age of 17 were accused of murder. That same year, 86 were murdered. In 1995, a record 111 juveniles were slain in Chicago.

It costs $16,000 a year to keep a person in prison, and it costs society $171,566 a year in injuries to the victim, plus indirect costs such as sales, taxes and educational opportunities.

The average murder sentence for rape is six years; average time served is 3.7 years.

Nearly 46 percent of the inmates released from Illinois prisons are incarcerated again within three years.

There are more than 1,000,000 people in prisons throughout the United States.

Review Questions

Test your knowledge about Chicago street gangs and drugs. For the correct answers, refer to the page number in parentheses.

1. How many street gangs are in Chicago? (page 3)

2. "Brothers" wear their hats in which position? (page 3)

3. What colors do they wear?   (page 3)

4. "Folks" wear their hats in which position? (page 3)

5. What colors do they wear?   (page 3)

6.   A six-point star is the symbol of which gang? (page 4)

7.   A five-point star is the symbol of which gang? (page 4)

8.   Gangster Disciples, Black Gangster Disciples, Spanish Disciples, Black Disciples belong to which faction?
    (page 4)

9. Latin Kings, Black Peace Stones, Vice Lords, Conservative Vice Lords, Four Corner Hustlers belong to which faction? (page 4)

10. What symbols are used by Brothers? (page 5)

11. What symbols are used by Folks?   (page 6)

12. What is a creation?   (page 7)

13. What is a service?   (page 7)

14. What is a blessing?   (page 8)

15. Name the common drugs in Caucasian communities? (page 63)

16. What is pollywog? (page 63)

17. What are the drugs commonly used in the African American community? (page 63)

18. What is ice? (page 64)

19. Thick, slurred speech, disorientation and impaired coordination are symptoms from use of which drugs? (page 70)

20. Agitation, elevated body temperature and hallucinations signal a possible overdose of which drugs? (pages 71-72)

21. What are some side effects of glue sniffing? (page 74)

22. What are some side effects from using LSD, PCP and Peyote? (pages 72-73)

23. How is cocaine stepped on? (pages 63-64)

24. How are heroin, cocaine and marijuana usually sold? (page 67)

25. What are some common inhalants? (page 74)

I have worked for CTA almost 13 years and during that time, I could remember 95th and the Dan Ryan was a tough place to work. But in the past year, one person has made a difference in the safety of the riders at 95th and the Dan Ryan. That person is a police officer by the name of Beckom.

When I first saw him making the kids put their hats straight, I thought he was trying to be another cop taking advantage of youths. But I soon found out that he had a program working to make the area safe because prior to his efforts, the kids who wore the hats to the right would fight the kids with the hats to the left. I later found out that red and black was a gang and that blue and black was another gang, and Officer Beckom was well informed about these gangs; so much so, in the past year he has worked at 95th and the Dan Ryan, I have seen him take about 20 handguns from the different kids coming through the station, not to mention knives and other weapons of destruction to human life.

Officer Beckom isn't just a good cop, but he really takes an interest in the kids and their growth. He also talks to the kids about pride in themselves and respect for others. There was a fight almost everyday or a shooting before Officer Beckom came to the station. I see Officer Beckom now has a partner, Officer Ross, who works along the same lines of communication with kids. Almost all the schools in the city come through the station from the West Side of Chicago and Far South.

I would think at least 50,000 kids a week and about 1,000,000 adults use the station, but Officers Beckom and Ross keep everyone safe from the bad guys. I would just like to have these two officers recognized and thanked for a job well-done. The job they are doing is really appreciated by the workers at the CTA station. Their work is also liked by the passengers that ride the buses and the trains on CTA everyday. The area of 95th and the Dan Ryan is now called peace land.

Chicago Defender Platform, article "Salutes Police" by
Joyce Jackson, citizen of Chicago

Nansen Elementary School is located at 12607 S. Union Ave. in the South Pullman area of Chicago. For quite some time, the neighborhood surrounding Nansen has been plagued by gangs and drug activity, as so many of our neighborhoods have been. However, unlike too many of our neighborhoods, this community is fortunate enough to have within its midst a strong, committed, involved parent who also happens to be a Chicago police officer.

Officer Beckom is the chairman of the Gang Prevention and School Planning and Beautification committees at Nansen School. He is also the chairman of the Youth Action committee of the African American Police League. He has recently begun implementation of what he refers to as his 4-Stage Program.

Stage 1 began March 8 at the Local School Council meeting, where Officer Beckom provided information to parents on indicators they should take heed of to determine whether or not their children are involved in gang activity.

Stage 2 began when he gave a presentation at Nansen to two eighth-grade classes on Violence and Adolescents. After this presentation, some expressed seeing visible changes in their children.

Stage 3 manifested itself in a field trip for eighth graders to the Cook County Jail at 2600 S. California Ave. Here, the students had an opportunity to witness persons during their incarceration as victims within the criminal justice system.

Stage 4 of the program took place recently at Nansen School's LSC meeting, at 7 p.m. At that meeting, specific guidelines were established for the community to follow in order to empower itself to counter and prevent the adverse behavior it has been experiencing. At the conclusion of the meeting, Officer Beckom presented an outline of activities for the youths to participate in during the summer.

Jesse Beckom's example of commitment to his community and people should serve as a positive one that each of us can receive inspiration and hopefully, motivation from. One or two Jesse Beckom's sprinkled here and there is not enough. But when individuals of this caliber come to the attention of those of us accomplishments with others. Take your bow, Officer Beckom. You deserve it and we are very proud of you.

Chicago Defender Platform, article "Parents, pride and community," by
Patricia Hill - president of the African American Police League

Dear Mr. Beckom:

Thank you for being a facilitator at our Alpha Lite Program Seminar "Gangs and Substance Abuse" held on November 4, 1995 at the campus of Elmhurst College, Science Center Building, in Elmhurst, Illinois. One hundred and fifteen parents and students attended the seminar and indicated a high level of enjoyment and a highly valued learning experience in reference to your participation.

Mu Mu Lambda Chapter also wishes to thank you for consenting to be part of our career awareness/youth motivation programs of our fraternity alumni chapter. Your participation is greatly appreciated because of your concern for today's African American youth and for that we commend you.

We look forward to seeing you again in the future. We hope that you can be part of the continuing program this year.

Sincerely yours,

Kenneth W. Brent
Director, Educational Activities
Mu Mu Lambda Chapter
Chicago Western Suburbs
Alpha Phi Alpha Fraternity Inc.

HOW MUCH DO YOU KNOW ABOUT GANGS, DRUGS AND VIOLENCE?

Now that you've read the book,
"GANGS, DRUGS AND VIOLENCE: CHICAGO STYLE,"
get some answers in person from author Jesse Beckom Jr. If you are an educator, principal, counselor, community leader, parent or simply a concerned citizen, you need to know how gangs, drugs and violence impacts your city, community and, possibly, your family.

Mr. Beckom conducts presentations for elementary and high schools, teacher in-service workshops, churches and community organizations. To arrange a presentation for your organization, call 312/821-6151.

GET ANSWERS FROM AN EXPERT !!!!

CALL TODAY

ORDER FORM

GANGS, DRUGS AND VIOLENCE:
CHICAGO STYLE
NOW AVAILABLE ON VIDEO!!!!

This eye-opening book is now available in a 60-minute video. Order a copy for your school, church, community organization and, most importantly, your family.

Save your children...Save your community!

(PLEASE TYPE OR PRINT)
Book only____Number of copies_____at $19.95 each
Video only___ Number of copies_____at $24.95 each
SAVE $10.00!! GET THE BOOK AND VIDEO FOR $39.95

Name_____

Organization_____
_____

Address_____
_____

City_____

State_____ **Zip**_____

Phone_____

Add $4.00 for shipping and handling

Make check or money order payable to:
Gangs, Drugs and Violence Prevention Consultants Inc.
P.O. Box 288833
Chicago, IL 60628-8833
"Respect in Self and Pride in the Community"